Dear Parents, Caregivers, and Educators:

This book presents everyday issues that all children face. On page 22, you'll find some questions to help children further explore these issues, both as they are presented in the story, and also as they might apply in the children's own lives. We hope these questions serve as starting points for developing a deeper understanding and appreciation of this book and the challenging situations it presents.

First American edition published in 2005 by
Picture Window Books
5115 Excelsior Boulevard
Suite 232
Minneapolis, MN 55416
877-845-8392
www.picturewindowbooks.com

First published in 2001 by
A & C Black (Publishers) Ltd
37 Soho Square
London WID 3QZ

Text copyright © Citizenship Foundation 2001
Illustrations copyright © Tim Archbold 2001

Published in conjunction with the Citizenship Foundation.
Sponsored by British Telecom.

Printed in the United States of America.

Library of Congress Cataloging-in-Publication Data
Rose, Gill, 1949-
The scary movie : a book about using good judgment / by Gill Rose ;
illustrated by Tim Archbold.
p. cm. — (Making good choices)
Summary: When Claire has trouble sleeping and has nightmares, she
is sorry that she watched a frightening video.
ISBN 1-4048-0663-6 (hardcover)
[1. Fear—Fiction. 2. Video recordings—Fiction. 3. Choice—Fiction.]
I. Archbold, Tim, ill. II. Title. III. Series.
PZ7.R7157Sc 2004
[E]—dc22   2004007470

The Scary Movie

by Gill Rose

illustrated by Tim Archbold

PICTURE WINDOW BOOKS
Minneapolis, Minnesota

The night Claire's uncle came to stay,
the grown-ups rented a movie to watch together.

Claire hoped that if she sat still and
kept quiet as a mouse, her mom and dad
might let her stay up and watch the movie with them.

It seemed to work.

No one noticed Claire sitting quietly in the corner.

She was very happy with herself ...

until she saw something SCARY on the movie
that made her feel really frightened.
Claire shut her eyes tight.

Whenever she opened her eyes to peep,
Claire saw horrible things happening
on the screen.

But even if she shut them again,
she could still hear the noises
and the scary music.

Claire didn't know what to do.

She could go to bed, but now she felt too scared to be upstairs by herself.

She could tell her mom and dad that she was scared, but they would probably get angry and send her to bed anyway.

What could she do?

Claire stayed where she was. For a little while, the
movie was just like a normal TV program.
Claire decided that she could handle this. She felt quite cool.

AAGH!

Just then, even the grown-ups screamed.

Claire buried her face in a pillow, her heart thumping.

But that didn't really help because she could imagine

what was happening, and that was scary, too.

At last, she could stand it no longer.
Trying not to make a sound,
Claire crept out of the room on her knees ...

and tiptoed up the stairs.

It was dark at the top of the stairs.
Claire turned the light on and felt a little braver.

She remembered to brush her teeth,
but she was too scared to look in the mirror,
in case she saw something coming up behind her.

Claire jumped quickly into bed before
anything nasty could grab hold of her ankles.

She had never felt so scared in her life!

When Mom and Dad looked in on their way to bed,
Claire was still sitting up, wide awake.

She asked them to leave the light on.
Mom and Dad couldn't understand why.

Claire lay there a long time thinking of all sorts of scary things.

That night Claire had real nightmares.
She woke up shouting for her mom and dad.

Mom and Dad came running into Claire's room.

Mom gave her a hug.

Dad said, "It's all right. It's only a dream."

But Claire wished she had not watched that movie!

Something to think about ...

- Was it all right for Claire to be watching the movie? Why or why not?

- Why do you think she wasn't in bed?

- Do you think Mom and Dad should have chosen a movie Claire could watch with them? Why or why not?

- What do you think her mom and dad would have done if they had found Claire hiding downstairs?

- What would you do if you were Claire's mom or dad? Why would you do that?

- Why didn't Claire tell her mom and dad that she was frightened?

- Talk about when it is fun to be a bit frightened and when being frightened is not fun.

- Why do you think there are some movies and TV programs that children are not allowed to watch?

- Would it be a good idea for Claire to tell Mom and Dad why she was feeling scared that night, or should she never talk about it? Why do you think so?

- Who can you go to for help if you are feeling scared or lonely? Think of as many people as you can.

Glossary

frightened—scared or afraid

normal—average or usual

screen—the front of a TV set

thumping—pounding

To Learn More

At the Library
Hirschmann, Kris. *Courage*. Chicago: Raintree
    Steck-Vaughn, 2004.
Pfister, Marcus. *Milo and the Magical Stones*. New York:
    North-South Books, 1997.
Vogel, Elizabeth. *Dealing with Choices*. New York:
    Powerkids Press, 2003.

On the Web
FactHound offers a safe, fun way to find Web sites related to this book.
All of the sites on FactHound have been researched by our staff.
www.facthound.com

1. Visit the FactHound home page.
2. Enter a search word related to this book, or type in this special code: 1404806636.
3. Click the FETCH IT button.

Your trusty FactHound will fetch the best Web sites for you!

Look for all of the books in this series:

Joe's Car

The Sandbox

The Scary Movie

William and the Guinea Pig